Testing English-Language Learners in U.S. Schools

Report and Workshop Summary

Committee on Educational Excellence and Testing Equity

Kenji Hakuta and Alexandra Beatty, *Editors*

NATIONAL RESEARCH COUNCIL

NATIONAL ACADEMY PRESS
Washington, D.C.

NATIONAL ACADEMY PRESS   2101 Constitution Avenue, N.W.   Washington, DC 20418

NOTICE: The project that is the subject of this report was approved by the Governing Board of the National Research Council, whose members are drawn from the councils of the National Academy of Sciences, the National Academy of Engineering, and the Institute of Medicine. The members of the committee responsible for the report were chosen for their special competences and with regard for appropriate balance.

This study was supported by Contract/Grant No. R305U960001-98A between the National Academy of Sciences and U.S. Department of Education. Any opinions, findings, conclusions, or recommendations expressed in this publication are those of the author(s) and do not necessarily reflect the views of the organizations or agencies that provided support for the project.

International Standard Book Number 0-309-07297-2

SUGGESTED CITATION: National Research Council (2000) *Testing English-Language Learners in U.S. Schools: Report and Workshop Summary*. Committee on Educational Excellence and Testing Equity. Kenji Hakuta and Alexandra Beatty, Editors. Board on Testing and Assessment, Center for Education. Washington, DC: National Academy Press.

Additional copies of this report are available from National Academy Press, 2101 Constitution Avenue, N.W., Lockbox 285, Washington, DC 20055; (800) 624-6242 or (202) 334-3313 (in the Washington metropolitan area); Internet, http://www.nap.edu

Printed in the United States of America

THE NATIONAL ACADEMIES

National Academy of Sciences
National Academy of Engineering
Institute of Medicine
National Research Council

The **National Academy of Sciences** is a private, nonprofit, self-perpetuating society of distinguished scholars engaged in scientific and engineering research, dedicated to the furtherance of science and technology and to their use for the general welfare. Upon the authority of the charter granted to it by the Congress in 1863, the Academy has a mandate that requires it to advise the federal government on scientific and technical matters. Dr. Bruce M. Alberts is president of the National Academy of Sciences.

The **National Academy of Engineering** was established in 1964, under the charter of the National Academy of Sciences, as a parallel organization of outstanding engineers. It is autonomous in its administration and in the selection of its members, sharing with the National Academy of Sciences the responsibility for advising the federal government. The National Academy of Engineering also sponsors engineering programs aimed at meeting national needs, encourages education and research, and recognizes the superior achievements of engineers. Dr. William A. Wulf is president of the National Academy of Engineering.

The **Institute of Medicine** was established in 1970 by the National Academy of Sciences to secure the services of eminent members of appropriate professions in the examination of policy matters pertaining to the health of the public. The Institute acts under the responsibility given to the National Academy of Sciences by its congressional charter to be an adviser to the federal government and, upon its own initiative, to identify issues of medical care, research, and education. Dr. Kenneth I. Shine is president of the Institute of Medicine.

The **National Research Council** was organized by the National Academy of Sciences in 1916 to associate the broad community of science and technology with the Academy's purposes of furthering knowledge and advising the federal government. Functioning in accordance with general policies determined by the Academy, the Council has become the principal operating agency of both the National Academy of Sciences and the National Academy of Engineering in providing services to the government, the public, and the scientific and engineering communities. The Council is administered jointly by both Academies and the Institute of Medicine. Dr. Bruce M. Alberts and Dr. William A. Wulf are chairman and vice chairman, respectively, of the National Research Council.

Contents

Preface

The Committee on Educational Excellence and Testing Equity was created under the auspices of the National Research Council (NRC), and specifically under the oversight of the Board on Testing and Assessment (BOTA). The committee's charge is to explore the challenges that face U.S. schools as they work to achieve the related goals of academic excellence and equity for all students. BOTA members recognized that an inevitable consequence of the heightened standards that are at the heart of current reforms is that some students will fail to meet them. As a result, BOTA wished to pay close attention to the consequences of these reforms. Of particular interest were the effects that new standards-based tests might have on students already at increased risk for school failure. BOTA members desired attention to be given not only to provisions made in reform programs to prepare *all* students for the new challenges, but also to the consequences for students who were unable to meet these higher goals. BOTA members were also concerned about the potential unintended consequences of reform efforts. The breadth and importance of these concerns led to the creation of a body that could devote its attention exclusively to these issues.

Thus, in 1998, the Forum on Educational Excellence and Testing Equity was formed. In its first two years this diverse and multidisciplinary body held a series of meetings and workshops to begin surveying the landscape of issues in its purview. At the end of that time the NRC leadership determined that there were a range of important ongoing issues for the forum to address, and that it should be empowered to draw conclusions and make recommendations to policy makers, educators, and researchers based on its findings. In the spring of 2000 the group was reconstituted as the Committee on Educational Excellence and Testing Equity.

This document reflects that transition in that it provides not only the summary of a workshop held by the forum on the testing of English-language learners (students learning English as an additional language) in U.S. schools, but also a report on the new committee's conclusions derived from that workshop and from subsequent deliberations. An important aspect of this committee's mission is to provide policy makers at all levels and others with succinct summaries of the state of research and practice on important topics. Because of its diversity both in expertise and perspective, the committee is well positioned to sift through matters of fact and opinion, and to provide thoughtful analysis for policy makers and others on the issues and debates that concern them.

While much has been written about the needs of English-language learners, there is an air of disarray in the discussion. Sometimes vehement disagreements about the value and fairness of different approaches to educating the growing population of English-language learners in the United States have partly obscured some important aspects of the education of these students. The forum turned its attention to the specific challenges of devising and administering suitable tests to achieve different purposes related to the needs of English-language learners. It considered the need for information about individual students' progress; needs for accountability data for schools, districts, and states; and the need to monitor broader trends in the educational progress of this group of students.

Subsequently, the new committee set aside time to weigh and discuss both the workshop presentations and discussions and other materials. The committee members identified several key messages from their review and present them here together with several recommendations to the field. The summary of the workshop fleshes out these findings with a more detailed picture of the issues. Our hope is that this short report will be of use to those who are actively engaged in addressing the needs of the approximately 3,000,000 children in our schools who are not fully proficient in English. The committee wishes to recognize the contributions of the many individuals who participated in the forum workshop, who are too numerous to list here (a list is included in Appendix A). Both their thoughtful discussions and the many supporting materials they supplied were very useful to the committee as it explored this complex topic and their participation has been much appreciated. Andrew Tompkins' able assistance with the report is gratefully acknowledged as well.

This report has been reviewed in draft form by individuals chosen for their diverse perspectives and technical expertise, in accordance with procedures approved by the NRC's Report Review Committee. The purpose of this independent review is to provide candid and critical comments that will assist the institution in making the published report as sound as possible and to ensure that the report meets institutional standards for objectivity, evidence, and responsiveness to the study charge. The review comments and draft manuscript remain confidential to protect the integrity of the deliberative process.

We wish to thank the following individuals for their review of this report: Jamal Abedi, Center for the Study of Evaluation, University of California, Los Angeles; Anne Hafner, Charter College of Education, California State University, Los Angeles; Charlene Rivera, Center for Equity and Excellence in Education, The George Washington University; Russell Rumberger, School of Education, University of California, Santa Barbara; and Wendy Yen, Consultant, Pebble Beach, California.

Although the reviewers listed above have provided constructive comments and suggestions, they were not asked to endorse the conclusions or recommendations nor did they see the final draft of the report before its release. The review of htis report was overseen by Richard Duran, University of California at Santa Barbara, appointed by the Center for Education, who was responsible for making certain that an independent examination of this report was carried out in accordance with institutional procedures and that all review comments were carefully considered. Responsibility for the final content of this report rests entirely with the authoring committee and the institution.

Eva Baker, *chair*
Board on Testing and Assessment

Introduction

B etween 1990 and 1997 the number of U.S. residents who were not born in the United States increased by 30 percent, from 19.8 million to 25.8 million, to reach the largest total in the nation's history (U.S. Census Bureau, 1999:2). Many in this population may be fluent English speakers, and many born in the United States may not be; nevertheless these numbers illustrate a significant challenge facing our public schools. Schools around the country have been struggling to keep up with the responsibility for educating sometimes rapidly shifting populations of students whose command of spoken and written English—and previous academic preparation—vary widely.

This challenge is not a new one, of course, for a country that has been the destination of waves of immigrants from all over the world in the course of its history, but the specific responsibilities facing states and districts today are shaped by current perspectives and circumstances. As the nation enters the twenty-first century, few question its responsibility to provide schooling for all children through high school, though this was not always the case. But in recent decades changing immigration patterns have heightened tensions around the question of how best to make room for new students in systems that are sometimes already highly stressed, and how best to educate students who are not already proficient in English. Most states have witnessed sharp disagreements about the pros and cons of different educational strategies for English-language learners—students somewhere along the road from understanding no English to being completely proficient.[1]

At a time when educational testing is a factor with ever-increasing impact on students' lives and on the fates of schools, districts, teachers, and administrators, it is not surprising that questions about how and when to test English-language learners, and what to make of their test scores, have been some of the most vexing ones. In discussions of these issues, the Forum on Educational Excellence and Testing Equity identified five specific questions about considerations that affect the testing of English-language learners to explore at a workshop held in October 1999.

• What is the best way to decide which English-language learners should be included in a given testing program?
• What is the best way to decide which accommodations are appropriate for English-language learners who are taking a particular test? [2]
• How might we evaluate the effects of accommodations on the results of a particular test?
• What should reports of test results convey about which students were included and about any accommodations that were provided? How might these reports vary depending on their intended recipients?
• What factors need to be considered in planning tests for different purposes, such as those for use in making high-stakes decisions about individual students or those used for system accountability?

---

[1]The term English-language learner is generally used in this report, following the practice adopted in a previous NRC report "Improving Schooling for Language-Minority Children." While other terms are used in some contexts, the committee responsible for that report chose the term that emphasizes these students' learning rather than their limitations. The term limited English proficient (LEP) is used when the context requires it. That term is defined in federal guidelines as "national origin minority students who cannot speak, read, write, or comprehend English well enough to participate meaningfully in and benefit from the schools' regular education program." (Office of Elementary and Secondary Education, 2000)

[2]Accommodations are changes "to the testing situation, (e.g.) presentation format, response format, setting, and the timing/scheduling of tests. [They are] a means of enabling [English-language learners] to demonstrate their academic knowledge despite their limited English proficiency." (Rivera *et al.*, 2000) A list of specific accommodations is provided on page 25.

These five questions provided the genesis for a workshop that was an opportunity to explore some of the factors that complicate decisions about testing English-language learners, and to hear about both the experiences of several states that have grappled with them in different ways and the perspectives of test publishers. Researchers, state- and local-level policymakers and administrators, representatives from advocacy groups, and others convened to consider the questions the forum members had raised.

When the forum was converted in the spring of 2000 to a standing committee—with expanded powers under NRC guidelines—it took another look at the results of that workshop and identified some key messages from its findings. In the course of several meetings, the committee developed its thinking about the issues raised and identified recommendations it wanted to make to researchers, educators, policy makers, and test developers. Part One is the committee's report of its findings; it describes what the committee saw as major messages and uses them to frame recommendations. Part Two summarizes the key points from the workshop and is organized around what might be described as common-sense questions about the testing of these students.

1

Committee Findings

O ne participant in the workshop summed up the most sobering, and paradoxical, set of messages that could be taken from the presentations and discussion to illustrate the difficulties facing policy makers. It is crucial, he noted, to include all students in testing designed to hold teachers and administrators accountable for the education they are providing these students.[3] However, testing students whose language skills are likely to significantly affect their test performance will yield inaccurate results, unless it is English-language skills that are being tested. Accommodations can help students demonstrate what they know, but they can easily be misapplied; inappropriately applied accommodations—that is, ones that are not well designed to suit the content or skills being measured— can distort test results. It is not fair or sensible to test students for high-stakes purposes unless they have truly been provided with the classroom supports they need and real opportunities to learn the material in question. On the other hand, in the absence of reasonable substitutes for such tests, excluding English-language learners from them can have negative effects on students' school careers as well because educators may not recognize and attend to the particular needs of students who are not included.

---

[3]The questions raised by excluding students from testing programs are not unique to English-language learners; they also pertain to students with disabilities and others.

While most participants clearly agreed that the goals can seem to conflict, and that there is no one obvious solution, others pointed out that "the perfect must not be the enemy of the good." As a number of workshop discussions demonstrated, a substantial amount of sound research and practice have already yielded important insights, not only about pitfalls but about the details of how students learn a second language, and about the factors that can make schooling and testing these youngsters more or less successful. Moreover, as one participant noted, Massachusetts, the first state to mandate that every bilingual student's progress in learning English be assessed every year, did so in 1971. The goal for this mandate was to ensure that the students were being adequately taught, but the state has not found an appropriate testing instrument for this purpose and has delegated this responsibility to the districts. The state's long wait for a perfect instrument, he argued, may not have been necessary since a variety of tools are available to help administrators track students' performance.

RESULTS FROM THE WORKSHOP

The workshop provided committee members with a clear picture of English-language learners in U.S. schools and some of the factors that affect both their educational needs and decisions about testing them. These are presented in detail in Part Two of this report and summarized here.

1. U.S. schools face a significant challenge in educating a growing population of immigrants and others who are not proficient in English. Spanish-background elementary students concentrated in high-poverty schools comprise the majority of these students.

2. A decades-long set of legal precedents, beginning with the Civil Rights Act of 1964, has led to a clear expectation that English-language learners be provided with the same educational opportunities as other students, and that they be held to the same academic standards as other students.

3. English-language learners' academic needs are complex and variable. They need to develop not only mastery of conversational English, but also mastery of the academic spoken and written English necessary to do the academic work for which they are ready. Accomplishing the latter takes four to seven years, on average. Moreover, while their English skills are developing they also need to continue to make progress in other subjects and to receive appropriate and challenging instruction that prepares them

to meet required standards. Disentangling students' progress in English from their academic performance in other areas is difficult because oral and written English are tools used in all kinds of academic work, but educators need effective ways of monitoring all aspects of these students' academic progress.

4. Current state and district policies regarding the inclusion of English-language learners in testing, the use of accommodations for these students, and other issues vary significantly across the country. Accommodations can be used to compensate for limitations in a student's English proficiency and thereby make it possible to collect valid information about that student's knowledge or skills. On the other hand, if misused, accommodations can render testing results inaccurate. The appropriateness of accommodations depends both on the particular language status of the student and on the purposes for which he or she is being tested.

5. Two very different kinds of information about English-language learners' linguistic progress are needed. Educators need to know which students lack proficiency in English and may need academic supports or need to be accommodated in or excluded from testing. They also need ways of monitoring these students' linguistic progress after they are identified as English-language learners.

The workshop discussions also yielded a clear sense that more research is needed in a number of areas related to the testing of English-language learners. The most pressing need identified was for more long-term studies that track the progress of students beyond their reclassification as proficient in English and removal from bilingual or English as a Second Language (ESL) programs. Several participants noted that statistical tracking of language-minority students is difficult and has been spotty. Those who drop out of school or move, for example, can disappear from record-keeping systems, and the progress of students who are never enrolled in such programs is similarly unrecorded. The absence of these students can make the statistical picture of the support system inaccurate. Moreover, since students are frequently moved out of language support programs before they are completely proficient in English, particularly academic English, studies of their academic performance, career trajectories, and continuing language development after leaving the program would be very useful. Greater understanding of the effects of different accommodations was also cited as an important need.

Committee members and workshop participants clearly articulated the sometimes frustrating tensions between the goals of including students in testing for the sake of system accountability and adhering to testing standards to ensure the accuracy of testing results. The seeming paradoxes, however, may be most acute when a test is used for more than one purpose. Including English-language learners in testing is often the only way to capture information about these students' progress that will enable administrators and policy makers to make informed decisions about their education. Because of past policies that excluded many of these students from testing, there is an unacceptable dearth of information about them. On the other hand, inappropriate testing only yields misleading information that can lead to incorrect decisions about individual students and mistaken assumptions about groups of students.

A point that was the theme of a 1999 NRC report offers an important corrective to the apparent dilemma posed by the testing of English-language learners. As *High Stakes: Testing for Tracking, Promotion, and Graduation* (National Research Council, 1999a) made clear, states and school districts can include English-language learners in large-scale assessments and use their scores for system accountability even in cases where it would be inappropriate to use such scores to make promotion or graduation decisions about individual students, as, for example, when students have not had an opportunity to acquire the knowledge and skills the tests measure. The particular concerns about fairness that are paramount in the individual testing context are not necessarily a hindrance to collection of the aggregated data that is needed for system accountability. (Even in the collection of such aggregated data, the inclusion of students with limited English proficiency may yield invalid results, depending on the circumstances. This point is discussed later in the report.) Many of the workshop discussions seemed to lead toward a shared sense that the real goal in testing English-language learners is to strike a workable, real-world balance tailored to particular circumstances—to find ways to have true accountability for the successful education of these students without letting assessments turn into punishments for students or teachers.

POINTS TO CONSIDER

Perhaps because the variations in student populations and local circumstances were raised so frequently during the workshop, attention centered on questions that could profitably be asked about specific testing programs to help educators achieve the hoped-for balance.

• *Is the assessment valid for the purpose for which it is being used?* Well designed tests have clearly articulated purposes, and using them in other ways—either selecting students for testing according to incorrect criteria or using the scores to make inferences for which they were not validated—is likely to yield inaccurate results. This point is of particular importance in the context of decisions about testing English-language learners. Validity can be affected in subtle ways by language deficiencies, and identifying the level of proficiency that makes including a student in a particular test fair is not straightforward.

• *What is known about the effects of particular accommodations being considered in the setting in question?* The useful question is not "are accommodations fair and effective?" but rather, "if we want to assess the mathematics skills of these students, with these levels of English proficiency, what accommodations might help us do so accurately?" Both research findings and the experiences of others who have faced similar situations can be of use in answering these kinds of questions.

• *What are the possible long-term implications of a particular policy?* While it is clear that a variety of real-world factors influence decisions about inclusion and accommodations, thoughtful consideration of possible long-term effects (such as effects on graduation rates, or the long-term impact of spending priorities, for example) can be a useful corrective to short-term political considerations. Imagining, for example, how a policy that is being contemplated might work in a district whose population of English-language learners doubles in the next 10 or 20 years could be a useful way of focusing on its possible unintended consequences.

The committee took note of Ursula Casanova's reminder to the group that while issues of inclusion and accommodation are sometimes similar for students with disabilities and English-language learners, it is important to recognize the differences as well. Being literate in two languages, she noted, is an academic advantage, perhaps one less valued in the United States than in other countries, but not a status to be penalized. Unfortunately, however, for many English-language learners in U.S. schools literacy in two languages is a goal, not a reality. Because the population of English-language learners is growing at a time when reliance on testing for many kinds of educational purposes is also growing, the importance of thoughtful planning for testing this population is greater than ever. Many new tests have been developed and used in the past decade or two, but not all of them are accomplishing their stated goals. The goals for testing have grown out of ambitious goals for teaching all students to high standards; the risk to be averted is that tests can have the effect of working against those ambitious goals if their misuse leads to poor educational decisions for some students.

RECOMMENDATIONS

The committee, having deliberated on what it heard at the workshop and on supplementary information, has identified three recommendations for ways of improving on current uses of tests and data related to English-language learners.

With regard to assessment, it is clear that educators and policy makers need information about language-minority students' developing skills in English *and* about their developing academic skills and knowledge in other subject areas. These two needs should be understood as distinct and addressed separately. Research suggests that doing so is a particular challenge because language skills are easily confounded with other constructs in testing (Abedi *et al.*, 1995). Nevertheless, these two needs can be addressed.

Recommendation 1: Researchers should continue to target the separate needs for improved ways of assessing the developing language skills of English-language learners and improved ways of assessing their academic progress, regardless of their level of proficiency in English. They should focus on improving or expanding existing assessment tools or creating new tools for both purposes. [4]

Recommendation 2: Test developers, educators, and policy makers should make better use of existing knowledge of how these areas can be assessed by, for example, taking pains to use assessments that avoid unnecessary linguistic complexity; adapting existing tests of English proficiency to assess incremental progress; using a variety of appropriate means to assess students' academic and linguistic progress; and avoiding inappropriate practices such as arbitrary cut-offs in the length of time that English-language learners can receive testing accommodations or other supports.

In part because of past policies of excluding English-language learners from large-scale data collection efforts, information about their educational status has been spotty and less reliable than it should be. The committee

---

[4] The committee notes that some work of this kind has already been undertaken.

recommends that the collection of data on these students be improved in several ways.

Recommendation 3: Policy makers and funding agencies should consider the need for consistent longitudinal data about the progress of English-language learners through school and beyond at both the national and state levels. Researchers, policy makers, and the public need valid information that yields insights into how these students fare whether or not they are enrolled in instructional programs that target their linguistic and cognitive needs as second-language learners. Information is also needed about English-language learners after they leave school and move into the workforce, and after they stop receiving any educational supports. More data are also needed to improve our understanding of variations in the kinds of bilingual services and testing accommodations children receive and their effects; how long they are eligible to receive them; and how their progress is affected by factors such as the age at which they entered the system.

It is the committee's hope that policies regarding the testing of English-language learners will grow more consistent and accurate as the ramifications of different approaches come to be better understood. Moreover, if data collection is improved and more is learned about the progress of these students through school, strategies for attending to their developing language skills and to their academic achievement should become more focused and successful than they are now.

2

Workshop Summary

Awealth of information was presented at the workshop on which much of this report was based. Researchers, legal experts, federal officials, state and local policy makers and administrators, and representatives from test publishers and advocacy groups all gathered to present and discuss the issues at hand. The material the committee has collected, from the presentations and materials supplied, the workshop discussions, and supplemental reading, is organized here in the form of discussions of some basic questions one might ask about the testing of English-language learners in U.S. schools.

WHO ARE THE ENGLISH-LANGUAGE LEARNERS IN OUR SCHOOLS?

The population of students for whom language is an issue is a particularly difficult one to characterize because it is extremely diverse and changing rapidly. Nationwide, more than six million school-age children, or 14 percent, live in homes where languages other then English are used. Of these children, about 45 percent are identified as Limited English Proficient (LEP), and need special assistance in school. Of the 14 percent, about three-fourths are from Spanish-speaking families and about three-fourths are poor and attend high-poverty schools. Five states, California, Texas, New York, Florida, and Illinois, are home to the majority of these students; indeed 40 percent of LEP students can be found in just 6 percent of school districts (National Center for Education Statistics (NCES), 1997:37-38).

Even within these high-concentration areas, many schools must adapt to rapid change. Committee member James Kadamus described the situation in New York State, which has identified 178,000 students in its system as English-language learners, 6 percent of its total student population. These students speak approximately 135 different languages and are heavily concentrated in the state's urban areas. New York's current policy is to use census and other data to calculate the five most populous language groups, and to offer bilingual programs in those languages. The tough part is that they must recalculate every year and quickly adapt their resources for the revised combination of languages.

The traditional destinations for immigrants—coastal cities, for example—are not the only jurisdictions that have been adjusting to rapid demographic shifts. Wausau, Wisconsin, a city that in 1980 was found by the U.S. Census to be "the most ethnically homogeneous city in the nation," is an example of a place that has experienced an unexpected but very rapid shift. A trickle of refugees who arrived in the late 1970s has increased to a population of about 4,200 (in a city of some 37,500), and the city's elementary school population is now 20 percent Asian (virtually all from the Hmong population). This rapid growth has strained the school system financially and required it to work quickly to develop bilingual programs (Stephenson, 1998:3, 4, and 8, Beck, 1994). Communities in many regions of the country have experienced similar changes, and, while population projections are far from foolproof, current predictions are that the percentage of the population that is of Hispanic origin will grow, immigration rates will remain constant, and the populations of elementary and secondary school-age children will fluctuate but increase overall by 2050 (U.S. Census Bureau, 1996:1-9, 29). Such projections, and the experience of communities such as Wausau, suggest that a closer look at policies for educating language minority children may move higher on the agenda in many communities.

While it is clear that a great deal of flexibility is required of U.S. schools, it is important to remember that at present one of the most pressing challenges educators face in this context—in terms of numbers—is that of educating Spanish-background elementary students concentrated in high-poverty schools. Native Spanish speakers make up approximately three-fourths of the population that has been identified as limited-English proficient (National Center for Education Statistics, 1997:39). As was noted above, the population of native Spanish speakers in schools is likely to increase. Demographers forecast that "If immigration and birth rates remain at current levels, the total Hispanic population will grow at least three times faster than the population as a whole for several decades" (Suro, 1998:6). Moreover, Hispanic students are the most highly segregated group in America's public schools—that is, most likely to attend schools with non-diverse populations—and their segregation is increasing (Orfield and Eaton, 1996:59).

The Hispanic population itself is quite diverse, representing many countries of origin and cultural traditions and a range in socio-economic status. Moreover, as a group, both Hispanic and other students who enter U.S. schools not proficient in English also bring with them a wide range of previous academic experience. Some are fully literate in their native languages and ready to plunge into content appropriate to their age and grade level. Others are not, and bring very different needs to the classroom (LaCelle-Peterson and Rivera, 1994:59). Over half of Hispanic students attend schools in which the majority of students are classified as low socio-economic status (McUsic, 1999). Nevertheless, the challenge of bringing native Spanish speakers, frequently from low-income families and with other sources of academic disadvantage, to proficiency in English, while maintaining their academic progress in all subjects, is one that schools and districts around the country face.

WHAT ARE THE LEGAL REQUIREMENTS?

One session of the workshop provided a review for workshop participants of the case law that has applied to the testing of English-language learners. BOTA member William Taylor began with a focus on Title I of the 1994 Elementary and Secondary Education Act (ESEA), which he described as "a bill of rights for English-language learners and other poor kids."[5] He observed that it explicitly requires states to hold LEP students

---

[5] The ESEA is legislation that extends the authorization of appropriations for educational programs of many kinds originally made under the ESEA of 1965. Title I of the ESEA (known during the 1980s as Chapter 1) is the section of the legislation that specifically addresses the needs of disadvantaged children. The 1994 legislation explicitly requires, for the first time, that—for Title I purposes—educational jurisdictions hold all students to the same performance standards and include them in the same assessment program regardless of their need for Title I services or other supports.

to the same high standards that apply to others, at least for Title I assessments, and that it calls for appropriate assessments and proper accommodations to be used to achieve this accountability. The legislation specifically requires

> ...the inclusion of limited English proficient students who shall be assessed, to the extent practicable, in the language and form most likely to yield accurate and reliable information on what such students know and can do, to determine such students' mastery of skills in subjects other than English (Office of Elementary and Secondary Education, 2000).

(It is important to note that the requirements of Title I are legally binding only on assessments conducted for purposes of Title I program accountability. Other testing conducted by states and districts, including many graduation and promotion exams, are not governed by these requirements.)

The basic requirement is for all students to be assessed, and for reasonable accommodations to be made for students with disabilities or limited English proficiency. Judith Johnson of the U.S. Department of Education described the specific implications for assessing LEP students, noting that states are required to identify the languages spoken by students within their systems and "make every effort to develop" assessments that can be used with these students (Office of Elementary and Secondary Education, 2000). They are required to consider either accommodations or native language testing to obtain test scores that are valid for the students for whom they are responsible, depending on the students' needs and the instruction they have received.[6] These requirements are qualified by the phrase "to the extent practicable" to allow states some leeway in addressing changing populations of non-native English speakers and other practical concerns. While some flexibility in strategies is allowed, states are required to apply their policies regarding accommodations consistently across districts and schools. States are required to include all LEP students in assessments (again this applies only to assessment programs used for Title I purposes), and must make a determination for each student of what form of testing, accommodations, or alternate language testing would yield the most valid and reliable results for that student. The content and performance standards against which LEP students are tested may not be less rigorous than those for other students, and LEP students must be tested at all of the grades included on the statewide testing system.

---

[6]See the footnote on page 25 for discussion of different kinds of native-language testing.

The Title I legislation builds on the development over several decades of legal standards that have affected the schooling of English-language learners, and the discussion of those developments properly begins with Title VI of the 1964 Civil Rights Act. According to Title VI, discrimination based on race, color, or national origin is prohibited. Title VI requires schools and districts to provide "equal educational opportunity" for students whose limited English proficiency "excludes them from effective participation in the educational program offered by the district." A Supreme Court case, *Lau v. Nichols, 414 U.S. 563 (1974)*, later followed up on this point, holding that "there is no equality of treatment merely by providing students with the same facilities, textbooks, teachers, and curriculum; for students who do not understand English are effectively foreclosed from any meaningful education."

Also in 1974, Congress enacted the Equal Educational Opportunities Act (EEOA), judicial interpretations of which made more explicit what states and school districts must do to enable LEP students to participate "meaningfully" in the educational programs they offer. These standards were used in a 1981 appeals court ruling, *Casteneda v. Pickard, 648 F. 2d 989 (5th Cir. 1981)*, which articulates three basic requirements for LEP programs. A 1991 policy statement from the Office of Civil Rights explains how the Casteneda case applies to possible violations of Title VI of the Civil Rights Act.[7] The policy statement notes that "Title VI does not mandate any particular program for instruction for LEP students," but goes on to say that such programs must be "recognized as sound by some experts in the field or [be] considered a legitimate experimental strategy," "[be] reasonably calculated to implement effectively the educational theory adopted by the school;" and "succeed[s], after a legitimate trial, in producing results indicating that students' language barriers are actually being overcome" (Assistant Secretary for Civil Rights, 1991:1).

These legal requirements illustrate an important aspect of civil rights law regarding education, that ". . . educational principles are, importantly, part and parcel of the legal inquiry, and they guide legal judgments about

---

[7]The Office of Civil Rights of the U.S. Department of Education is the federal agency charged with enforcement of civil rights law as it pertains to education. Its policy statements describe the legal standards and court precedents that are relevant to particular issues and are designed to assist policy makers and others in adhering to the law.

high-stakes tests." (Coleman, 1998). Arthur Coleman and Judith Johnson of the U.S. Department of Education both spoke about the federal perspective on the requirements regarding English-language learners. Both observed that the details of policy implementation and the manner in which general principles are applied to specific local circumstances are the critical determinants of how successful a policy will be and the extent to which it will be in compliance with federal regulations.

Workshop participants concurred, noting that the legal standards, while crucial for holding educators responsible for adhering to important goals, provide only a framework in which to make the complex decisions policy makers face. A number of participants reminded the group that educators face decisions every day that either are not straightforward under the laws as framed, or must be made in a context that makes achieving the goals framed by the laws, and by researchers and other experts, extremely difficult.

WHAT ARE THE ACADEMIC NEEDS
OF ENGLISH-LANGUAGE LEARNERS?

Committee member Kenji Hakuta made a presentation at the workshop on the current state of knowledge about the academic needs of English-language learners. A primary distinction to make in characterizing this student population, he pointed out, is that between oral language mastery and academic language mastery. Researchers who have studied language acquisition use a variety of methods to measure proficiency with oral and written language. Using these measures as well as case studies of children and adults learning a second language, researchers have noted that while people can often learn basic conversational skills quite quickly, close study of their speech reveals that it typically takes three to five years for them to develop true oral proficiency, to use "the elaborate, syntactically and lexically complex code of the proficient language user" (quoted in Hakuta, Butler, and Witt, 1999:3).

Developing what researchers call academic English proficiency takes even longer, four to seven years, on average (Hakuta, Butler, and Witt, 1999). By academic English proficiency the experts mean the capacity to use spoken and written English with sufficient complexity that one's performance in an academic setting is not impaired. By this definition, however, academic English proficiency is not fixed but is understood in relation to the academic expectations that confront a particular learner at a particular age.[8] Defining academic English proficiency is also complicated by other factors, most notably socio-economic ones. Indeed, disentangling the effects of limited English proficiency on a student's learning and performance from the effects of other factors is not easily done. Family environment, poverty, and uneven teacher quality are just a few of the factors that can influence performance and these factors are particularly likely to affect the language-minority population because, as was noted above, their poverty rate is high relative to that of the population as a whole.

Researchers and others have recognized that isolating language as a factor is both important and difficult, and that detailed understanding of students' language skills as they progress toward proficiency is very important. NRC committees and others have recommended that students be evaluated regularly so that their teachers can modify their educational programs as they progress (National Research Council, 1999a, 1999b). Tests of language proficiency exist for this purpose, but many focus on grammatical structure and technical mastery, and recent research on bilingual competence has lead to the development of other means of evaluating students' language, including oral interviews, teacher checklists, and story re-telling. Many educators have also adopted portfolio assessments as a way of monitoring language growth, though most of these newer methods are more difficult to standardize and administer than traditional ones, for obvious reasons (National Research Council, 1997:117). The key here may not be the particular means by which students' progress is monitored, but the extent to which educators perceive learning spoken and written English as a variable and gradual process rather than one with defined stages and timelines that apply equally to all students. A particular point that emerged from the discussion was that educators and administrators need to recognize and plan for the time needed for students to achieve both oral and written fluency and the ability to operate in the school system without supports.

The complexity of defining these students may seem very confusing for officials who must find ways to classify large numbers of students for academic placement and testing, but understanding the stages of students'

---

[8]Indeed, as the linguistic demands of schooling increase, many English-language learners, even those who have been identified as "proficient" in elementary school, may need continued support and instruction to develop the advanced proficiency required for secondary- and college-level study.

progress toward fluency is important. The duration of bilingual programs is often based on the length of time a student has lived in the United States, attended a U.S. school, or been offered particular programs. In California, for example, the law limits the time for special language-related services to "a temporary transition not normally intended to exceed one year" (Proposition 227, Article 2, Sec. 305). After that time is expired, students are asked, with some exceptions, to function in an English-only setting regardless of their level of English proficiency. Arbitrary timelines, it was noted, have little relationship to the learning trajectory students must travel; such cutoffs generally allow little adjustment for individual circumstances and are unlikely to serve all, or even most, students' needs.

WHAT ABOUT TESTING?

Decisions about what kinds of testing are suitable for particular students or groups of students can seem equally arbitrary but are equally important. Rules and policies governing the inclusion of language-minority students are far from uniform from state to state, and across different kinds of testing programs. They also change frequently as states adjust to population changes, political shifts, and emerging evidence from both research and practice. Moreover, as Charlene Rivera noted at the workshop, many state policies are those that have been developed for children with disabilities and do not reflect a clear focus on the needs of English-language learners. Some states use proficiency measures to determine which students should be included, while others use a combination of criteria, such as number of years in the state's system, test scores, school performance, and teacher judgment (National Research Council, 1997:119). Currently, of the 49 states that use statewide assessments, one has no policy on inclusion in or exemption from the test and two allow no exemptions (that is, they require all students to participate regardless of their linguistic status). The remaining 46 states include English-language learners in testing after a certain amount of time in the system. Eleven states allow a two-year delay in testing, twenty-one states allow three years, two states allow more than three, and one state has no time limit (Rivera *et al.*, 2000).

One basic tension around the question of identifying appropriate policies is between the benefits that may come from having test results for particular students and the harm that may come from having results that are inaccurate. Like almost any issue involving educational testing, this one is best understood in the context of specific circumstances. Educators know that many different tests exist for many different purposes, and the cost-benefit analysis may look somewhat different depending on the purpose.

The principal purposes for educational tests are well known:

• *Accountability*—providing evidence of the performance of teachers, administrators, schools, districts, or states, relative to established standards or benchmarks, or in comparison to others, or both.

• *Decisions about students*—providing data that is used in making important decisions about individual students, such as placement in academic programs, grade promotion, or graduation.

• *Program evaluation*—providing evidence of the outcome of a particular educational program in terms of student performance.

• *Tracking of long-term trends*—providing evidence of changes in the performance of groups of students, such as those enrolled in a particular grade, school, or school district, or those belonging to population subgroups, etc.

• *Diagnosis*—providing information about students' strengths and weaknesses with regard to specific material or skills (such as proficiency in English, for example), for use in improving teaching and learning.

Each of these purposes can be achieved only if the test is valid for the particular purpose for which it is being used, and it is important to note that tests valid for one purpose may be invalid for others (National Research Council, 1999a). Measurement experts are in clear agreement that the validity of test results—and the accuracy of judgments based on those results—are seriously impaired if test-takers' performance is affected by factors other than their knowledge of the material being tested. Thus, for example, if a test is needed to determine how much students know about mathematics, its results will be invalid if the test-takers' limited English proficiency prevents them from understanding all of the questions, presenting their answers, or completing the work in the allotted time. In other words, a test cannot provide valid information about a student's knowledge or skills if a language barrier prevents the students from demonstrating what they know and can do.

For an individual student, being tested in a language in which he or she is not proficient will mean incorrect assessment of his or her knowledge or skills unless appropriate accommodations are used. Such incorrect assessments, especially when used to support high-stakes decisions about a student's education, can have lasting effects on his or her academic progress. For example, students who are incorrectly placed in an academic track or retained in grade because of a misused assessment may be increasingly susceptible to school failure or dropping out as a result (National Research Council, 1999a). Language issues can also make it difficult to assess the achievement of particular groups of students. The aggregate performance of language subgroups that are inappropriately tested can be seriously misunderstood, and decisions influenced by invalid test results can have significant impact on their lives.

The changing policies on including English-language learners in national tests and surveys illustrate this point. The National Assessment of Educational Progress (NAEP), for example, for many years excluded many English-language learners from testing, as did the National Education Longitudinal Study (NELS).[9] (Since 1995 NAEP has followed new guidelines and included more of these students.) The difficulty with such policies was that under them the useful data collected about English-language learners were limited. Since those students selected for testing were generally those most proficient in English, only a modest proportion of all English-language learners were tested, and the data were skewed, reflecting the performance of the most proficient subset of these students. In general, English-language learners have been excluded from testing because of the difficulty of obtaining valid measures of their performance. However, in response to the call for information about how well all students are progressing toward standards, progress has been made in recent years in improving on existing assessment instruments and procedures for English-language learners.

Measurement experts may have improved their understanding about the testing practices needed to achieve valid results, but a variety of factors place pressure on the educators who decide which students to include on various tests. As was made clear at the workshop, policy makers and administrators know that following best practice guidelines can be complicated in the real world for a variety of reasons.

---

[9]NAEP is a large-scale assessment administered to randomly selected samples of 4th, 8th, and 12th graders to determine their knowledge and skills in selected subjects, including reading, mathematics, and science. NELS is a longitudinal survey through which data about U.S. students' progress through school are collected.

Educators do not have sufficient effective tools for classifying students at various levels of English proficiency. Without these it can be very difficult to identify the point at which students are ready to participate in a particular test. The methods that are used to identify English-language learners include reviewing registration and enrollment records; conducting home language surveys, interviews, and observations; and using referrals, classroom grades and performance, and test results (National Center for Education Statistics, 1997:36). Researchers have found that test results are the most common means (LaCelle-Peterson and Rivera, 1994:65). Nevertheless, there is currently not a detailed, universally accepted definition of English-language learners.

Two key points about the necessary tools emerged at the workshop. First, two very different kinds of information about English-language learners' progress are needed. Educators need to know not only which students lack proficiency in English and who may need academic supports, but also which students need to be accommodated in or even excluded from testing. They also need ways of monitoring these students' progress after they are identified as English-language learners. As noted above, it typically takes an English-language learner three to seven years to develop full academic proficiency and to be ready to be reclassified (as no longer needing language supports). Teachers and administrators need ways of making sure that these students' language skills are improving throughout the time they are classified as English-language learners so they can ensure the students are receiving the support they need.

A separate but related need is for data about the progress of these students as a group. Schools and districts need to be held accountable for how well they are helping these students progress, not just because it's a good idea but also because doing so is required by law. To monitor their own progress and the effectiveness of their programs, these jurisdictions need more information than tests that identify students as English-language learners or reclassify them as mainstream students can provide.

Virtually all educational tests rely to some extent on language skills, regardless of what they were designed to measure, and some rely very heavily on them. While educators may appreciate the importance of measuring academic skills on their own, irrespective of language skills, doing so can be difficult. Research by Jamal Abedi, who presented at the workshop, and others has shown that proficiency in English is strongly related to performance on a test of mathematics, and that reducing the linguistic complexity of test questions and instructions can yield higher performance in all groups (not only those for whom English is a second language), and particularly among lower ability students (Abedi *et al.*, 1995). Educators who work with English-language learners need ways of distinguishing their academic progress from their developing language skills so they can identify any problems with academic skills and content early. Aggregated data on these students' academic achievement, as distinct from their language status, is also needed, both for accountability purposes and to help educators evaluate their own programs.

Political pressures can be difficult to ignore. When educators or schools are held accountable for students' achievement, for example, there may be pressures to exclude English-language learners from large-scale assessments in order to boost pass rates. Excluding English-language learners from assessments aimed at system accountability, however, can mean that those students' needs will be unrecognized, and even that resources they need will not be allocated to them. Choosing not to include students who are less likely to perform well on an accountability test—and, as noted, language-minority students are frequently in that category for reasons other than language—can also be a way of shaping the results of tests that can have significant implications for schools, districts, and, increasingly, individual teachers and administrators.

Decisions about appropriate testing are closely tied to questions about the instruction students have received and the opportunities they have had to learn particular material and academic skills. While a full discussion of the many kinds of academic programs that are offered to English-language learners is beyond the scope of this report, it is clear that they vary widely. To the extent that English-language learners have not been taught the same material as mainstream students, or have been held to different standards, those circumstances need to be factored into decisions about what testing makes sense for those students. In practice, researchers have found that language minority students frequently either do not have access to all of the courses other students do, are placed in less demanding academic tracks, are not taught by teachers trained to work with English-language learners, or are taught by less experienced or able teachers (LaCelle-Peterson and Rivera, 1994, National Research Council, 1999a). Committee member Jay Heubert reminded the group of professional standards in this area. The American Psychological Association's (APA) *Joint Standards* assert that promotion and graduation tests should cover only the "content and skills that students have had an opportunity to learn" (AERA, APA, and NCME, 1999:146, Standard 13.5). The NRC's *High Stakes* reached a similar conclusion: "Tests should be used for high-stakes decisions...only after schools have implemented changes in teaching and curriculum that ensure that students have been taught the knowledge and skills on which they will be tested" (National Research Council, 1999a). The American Educational Research Association also, in a July 2000 *Policy Statement Concerning High Stakes Testing*, recommends that "[w]hen content standards and associated tests are introduced as a reform to . . . improve current practice, opportunities to access appropriate materials . . . should be provided before . . . students are sanctioned for failing to meet the new standards." (AERA, 2000:2)

Rebecca Zwick of the University of California at Santa Barbara made several important points at the workshop in this context. Noting that policy makers' dilemmas about testing are often intensified by the fact that different advocacy groups may be pushing in different directions, she also reminded the group that the testing purpose should be the key to decisions about inclusion. She reinforced the critical distinction between tests that yield individual scores and those designed to measure the performance of groups. Zwick also noted that performance assessments have been proposed as alternatives to traditional tests that seem to be less susceptible to group differences. She maintained that group differences are often actually larger with such tests because they impose heavy language burdens on test takers. Her conclusion was that while testing should be done thoughtfully, many of the problems associated with it are actually symptoms of wider problems. Schools in high-poverty areas, as many with large concentrations of English-language learners are, for example, frequently lack important educational resources by comparison with other schools in wealthier areas (Levin, 1996:229).[10] When such schools are staffed by less experienced teachers, have deteriorating or inferior physical plants, and have other significant disadvantages, the problems associated with testing their English-language learners are compounded. Conversely, if resource alloca-

---

[10]Levin notes in this chapter from an earlier NRC report that although there are clearly schools that are "seriously underfunded," "Adequate resources are a necessary condition for meeting the educational needs of at-risk populations but not a sufficient condition."

tion and other factors were in place to produce better learning for all students, some of the differences associated with testing could be ameliorated.

WHAT ABOUT ACCOMMODATIONS?

Educators have devised a variety of test accommodations—means by which the disadvantages students who are not proficient in English face in testing can be at least partially compensated for. Accommodations have become more frequently used as educators have focused on the need for information about how English-language learners are faring. A successful accommodation is a way of improving the accuracy of the information collected by the test and an important way of addressing the tension between the goals of inclusion and accuracy. However, there are a number of pitfalls in their use, and when one considers the variety that characterizes the population of English-language learners, this is not surprising.

As is the case with inclusion policies, states' policies on accommodation vary widely (Rivera *et al.*, 2000). Of the 49 states with tests, 40 have a policy and 37 allow accommodations. Among those that allow accommodations, there is considerable variation. The most commonly used methods of accommodating language minority students' needs include

- allowing extra time, extra breaks, or other flexibility in scheduling;
- administering the test in small groups;
- simplification or translation of directions;
- use of dictionaries or glossaries;
- reading of questions aloud or allowing students to dictate answers or use a scribe;
- assessing in students' native language or allowing students to respond in their native language;[11]
- allowing students to choose either English or native-language versions of test questions;

---

[11]It is important to note that "assessing in students' native language" can mean either administering a "parallel" version of an English language test or administering a different test, in the native language, that targets the same or closely related constructs as the original English version of the test. The latter case is considered not an accommodation but a different assessment. The parallel test might be developed along with the English version or translated from it, although observers have noted the many difficulties inherent in translating tests (Kopriva, 2000).

- administration of the test by a person familiar with test-takers' primary language and culture (National Research Council, 1997:119).

Each of these accommodations was devised in response to specific notions of English-language learners' needs, but particular ones may be suitable in some settings but not others. Indeed, as Charlene Rivera noted, many of these accommodations are prohibited in some states and allowed in others, or prohibited or allowed only on certain components of assessments. The probable reason for the variety—and the source of potential problems—may lie in the challenge of targeting the accommodation to the specific needs of particular students and the knowledge or skills being assessed. Some of the important factors to be considered in matching accommodations to particular testing situations that were discussed at the workshop include the following:

- *It is important to ensure that accommodations offered for a particular test do not affect its validity—that is, that they allow the student to be tested on the intended content—and are appropriate for the students tested.* As noted above, it can be difficult to disentangle English language skills from other academic skills. Some accommodations have the potential to give the students who are offered them an advantage over native English speakers, though the goal is only to provide an equal chance for all students to demonstrate their knowledge of the subject matter being assessed.
- *It is important to ensure that the accommodations used actually address the students' needs—and do not introduce other kinds of problems.* Providing a glossary for use during testing, for example, might be ideal for students who have experience with them and have a clear sense of how to use them in a testing situation. For others, the glossary may be a confusing, time-consuming distraction that may depress their performance.
- *The appropriateness of an accommodation needs to be carefully evaluated in the context of the testing purpose.* Different accommodations may be appropriate for the same students depending on what particular information is being sought. For example, the heavy language demands in testing a student's knowledge of history may require a different approach than would the relatively lesser linguistic demands in testing mathematics skills. Different approaches might well also be called for depending on whether the test was designed for use in academic placement or in a system accountability test.

- *Accommodations need to be considered in the context of instruction.* For example, if students have not been instructed in Spanish, testing them in Spanish is unlikely to yield valid information about their performance.

These goals reflect well established principles of measurement (as articulated in the APA *Joint Standards* and elsewhere, for example), but it is important to note that actually accomplishing them is easier said than done. Two earlier NRC reports have taken note of the fact that "Research that can inform policy and guidelines for making decisions about exemptions, modifications, and accommodations in assessment procedures is urgently needed" (National Research Council, 1997, 1999a). The committee is well aware of the practical difficulties that face those who need to make decisions about appropriate use of accommodations and hopes that these observations will be useful in the absence of more conclusive research findings.

DIFFERENT APPROACHES

States and districts around the country are currently addressing their English-language learners' needs in very different ways, and little formal research has been done to develop a clear national picture of how these students are tested, or how the policies relate to actual practice. Representatives from several jurisdictions described their policies and programs at the workshop.

Philadelphia. Because Pennsylvania has very limited legislation regarding English-language learners, the city of Philadelphia has developed comprehensive English for Speakers of Other Languages (ESOL) and bilingual programs organized under a central Office of Language Equity Issues. Mary Ramirez, the director of that office, described for the workshop the city's assessment policies for English-language learners. Philadelphia uses the Stanford Achievement Test-9th Edition (SAT-9), a commercially available achievement test based on national standards developed by professional societies and other national groups, and Apprenda 2, a Spanish-language version of the SAT-9.

The city's policy is to test virtually all students but they have identified three ESOL levels, and those identified through an evaluation process as beginners are excluded from testing. Certain accommodations are permitted for all English-language learners tested, depending on their proficiency level and the subject being tested, and these are described in public documents. The principles guiding the city's accommodation policies are described in the supporting documents as follows:

- The testing situation should not be the first time the student encounters an accommodated strategy.
- For students with disabilities, the testing accommodation should parallel the instructional accommodation as described in the IEP [Individualized Education Plan].
- For English-language learners, accommodation should result in enhanced comprehension of the test directions and questions (School District of Philadelphia, 1999:10).

Philadelphia has also taken seriously the responsibility of tracking their results and have test results that can be disaggregated by gender and ethnicity and also by ESOL proficiency level and by native language.

California. Sonia Hernandez of the California Department of Education provided a brief history of the numerous changes that have occurred in California's policies regarding English-language learners recently. (The information Hernandez presented has been supplemented by information available on the state's website, http://star.cde.ca.gov/.) Having dropped the California Learning Assessment System (CLAS), California has a new testing program, the Standardized Testing and Reporting Program, or STAR. This program incorporates the SAT-9, a commercially produced Spanish language test, the Spanish Assessment of Basic Education (SABE), which will provide information about English-language learners' reading, language, and mathematics skills. The approximately 2,000,000 English-language learners in the system all take the SAT-9 and are also required to take the SABE if they have been enrolled in California public schools for less than 12 months (that test is used at the discretion of the district after 12 months). The state is also developing a test of English Language Development (ELD), based on existing standards, which will assess students' English listening comprehension, speaking, reading, and writing. A high school exit examination in language arts and mathematics is currently being developed, as are mandatory tests linked to the optional state standards.

Hernandez noted that the passage of Proposition 227 has greatly complicated the testing situation for English-language learners since it has meant a significant drop in native-language instruction for these students as well as a sharp increase in recommendations that they be placed in Special Education programs. Ms. Hernandez noted that many in the state have been advocating that changes be made to improve the coherence of the state's various testing initiatives. She noted also that data collection efforts need to be improved so that the state can better track its English-language learners, and be held accountable for their performance.

References

Abedi, J., C. Lord, and J.R. Plummer

    1997   Final Report of Language Background as a Variable in NAEP Mathematics Performance. CSE Tech. Rep. 429. Los Angeles, CA: National Center for Research on Evaluation, Standards, and Student Testing (CRESST), University of California.

American Education Research Association

    2000   *AERA Position Statement Concerning High-Stakes Testing in PreK-12 Education.* Available: http//www.aera.net.about/policy/stakes.htm.

American Educational Research Association, American Psychological Association, and National Council on Measurement in Education

    1999   *Standards for Educational and Psychological Testing.* Washington, DC: American Psychological Association.

Assistant Secretary for Civil Rights

    1991   Memorandum from Michael L. Williams: Policy Update on Schools' Obligations Toward National Origin Minority Students with Limited-English Proficiency (LEP). Washington, DC: U.S. Department of Education, http://www.ed.gov/offices/OCR/lav1991.html.

Beck, R.

    1994   The ordeal of immigration in Wausau. *The Atlantic Monthly* 273 (4) (April): 84-97.

Coleman, A.L.

    1998   Excellence and equity in education: High standards for high-stakes tests. *Virginia Journal of Social Policy & the Law* 6 (1): 80-110.

Hakuta, K., Y.G. Butler, and D. Witt

    1999   *How Long Does It Take English-Language Learners to Attain Proficiency?* Unpublished manuscript. Stanford University, CA.

Kopriva, R.

2000   *Ensuring Accuracy in Testing for English-Language Learners.* Washington, DC: Council of Chief State School Officers, SCASS LEP Consortium.

LaCelle-Peterson, M.W., and C. Rivera

1994   Is it real for all kids? A framework for equitable assessment policies for English-language learners. *Harvard Educational Review* 64 (1) (Spring): 55-75.

Levin, H.M.

1996   Economics of school reform for at-risk students. Chapter 11 in *Improving America's Schools: The Role of Incentives,* E.A. Hanushek and D.W. Jorgenson, eds. Board on Science, Technology, and Economic Policy, National Research Council. Washington, DC: National Academy Press.

McUsic, M.

1999   The law's role in the distribution of education: The promises and pitfalls of school-finance litigation. In Heubert, J., ed., *Law and School Reform: Six Strategies for Promoting Educational Equity.* New Haven: Yale University Press.

National Center for Education Statistics

1997   *The Inclusion of Students With Disabilities and Limited English Proficient Students in Large-Scale Assessments: A Summary of Recent Progress.* (NCES 97-482).

National Research Council

1997   *Improving Schooling for Language-Minority Children: A Research Agenda.* D. August and K. Hakuta, eds. Committee on Developing a Research Agenda on the Education of Limited-English-Proficient and Bilingual Students, Board on Children, Youth, and Families, National Research Council. Washington, DC: National Academy Press.

1999a *High Stakes: Testing for Tracking, Promotion, and Graduation.* J.P. Heubert and R.M. Hauser, eds. Committee on Appropriate Test Use, Board on Testing and Assessment, National Research Council. Washington, DC: National Academy Press.

1999b *Testing, Teaching, and Learning: A Guide for States and School Districts.* R.F. Elmore and R. Rothman, eds. Committee on Title I Testing and Assessment, Board on Testing and Assessment, National Research Council. Washington, DC: National Academy Press.

Office of Elementary and Secondary Education, U.S. Department of Education

2000   *Summary Guidance on the Inclusion Requirement for Title I Final Assessments.* (April 4, 2000).

Orfield, G. and S. Eaton

1996   *Dismantling Desegregation: The Quiet Reversal of Brown v. Board of Education.* New York: The New Press.

Rivera, C., C. Stansfield, L. Scialdone, and M. Sharkey

2000   *An Analysis of State Policies for the Inclusion and Accommodation of English Language Learners in State Assessment Programs During 1998-1999.* Arlington, VA: The George Washington University, Center for Equity and Excellence in Education.

School District of Philadelphia

1999   *Assessment Accommodations Booklet,* taken from *A Helpful Guide to Standards Based Assessment.* Philadelphia, PA: Office of Assessment.

Stephenson, C.
    1998 Hmong change land that's changing them. *Milwaukee Journal Sentinel* (August 22).

Suro, R.
    1998 *Strangers Among Us: How Latino Immigration is Transforming America.* New York, NY: Alfred A. Knopf.

U.S. Census Bureau
    1996 *Population Projections of the United States by Age, Sex, Race, and Hispanic Origin: 1995 to 2050.* Current Population Reports, P25-1130. Washington, DC: U.S. Department of Commerce.
    1999 *Profile of the Foreign-Born Population in the United States: 1997.* Current Population Reports, P23-195. Washington, DC: U.S. Department of Commerce.

APPENDIX
A
Workshop Agenda and Participants

INCLUSION, ACCOMMODATION, AND REPORTING FOR ENGLISH-LANGUAGE LEARNERS IN STANDARDS-BASED REFORM

October 14-16, 1999
SRI International
Menlo Park, California

States and districts across the nation are pressing for rigorous standards of learning and for large-scale assessments that measure the progress of all students toward high levels. However, students for whom English is a second language often are excluded from standards-based assessment programs. Such exclusions can call into question the assessment results of schools and jurisdictions. Differential exclusion rates can also lead to invalid comparisons across states and among districts. Most importantly, exclusion removes English-language learning students from accountability systems and may threaten their access to the full benefits of educational reform.

This workshop is designed to review current research and practice on the inclusion and accommodation of English-language learning students in standards-based reform. Participants will discuss the social policy goals, legal protections, standard and assessment practices, and the outcomes of high-stakes tests for English-language learning students and for their schools.

Thursday, October 14, 1999

8:30-8:45　**Welcome and Introductions**

Ulric Neisser, Cornell University
Forum Co-Chair

William Trent, University of Illinois
Forum Co-Chair

Dennis Beatrice, SRI International

8:45-9:45　**Population Characteristics, Social Goals, and Educational Treatments for English-Language Learning Students**

Moderator—James Kadamus,
NY State Department of Education

Kenji Hakuta
Stanford University

• What terminology is used to designate students for whom English is a non-native language?
• What are the language backgrounds and family characteristics of these students?
• What social and educational goals have been articulated for English-language learning students in American schools?
• What are the educational backgrounds and what is the character and quality of the educational services provided to English-language learners?

9:45-10:15　Discussion

10:15-10:30　Break

Current Policy and Practice on the Inclusion and Accommodation of English-Language Learning Students

10:30-11:30   *Charlene Rivera*
                   GWU Center for Equity and Excellence in Education

• What criteria are used to determine whether English-language learners are included in state testing programs?
• How long are English-language learners exempted from state assessment programs?
• What accommodation strategies do states use (modifications of tests and testing procedures)?
• Do states prohibit provision of specific accommodations?
• What criteria are used to determine individual accommodations?
• Who makes decisions about individual accommodations?
• What domains are addressed (subject-matter knowledge, native language and literacy, English language and literacy, cognitive abilities)?
• What assessment purposes are being served (instructional planning, system-level monitoring and accountability, program placement or exit)?

11:30-12:00   Discussion

12:00-12:45   Lunch

Recent Research and Recommendations on the Inclusion and Accommodation of English-Language Learners

Moderator—Jay Heubert, Columbia University

12:45-2:15   Research on Inclusion, Accommodation, and Reporting for English-Language Learners

Jamal Abedi
University of California Los Angeles, CRESST

Inclusion and Testing of Limited-English-Proficient Students in Large-Scale Assessment

Richard Duran
University of California, Santa Barbara

Findings of the NRC Committee on Title I Testing

Ursula Casanova
Arizona State University

- What inclusion and accommodation practices for English-language learners are best supported by research?
- What domains are well addressed by current measures (assessment of subject-matter knowledge, native language and literacy, English language and literacy, cognitive abilities)?
- What assessment purposes are well served by current methods (instructional planning, system-level monitoring and accountability, program placement or exit)?
- What is known about the validity of score interpretations for English-language learning students in standards-based testing?
- What are the most pressing development and research questions?

2:15-2:45   Discussion

2:45-3:00   Break

3:00-3:45   **Inclusion and Accommodation for Students with Disabilities**

       Martha Thurlow
       University of Minnesota

       • What do we know about the inclusion and accommodation of students with disabilities in standards-based reform?
       • Do these practices hold promise for the education and assessment of English-language learning students?

3:45-4:30   **Federal Protections for English-Language Learning Students**

       Moderator—Diana Pullin, Boston College

       William Taylor
       Board on Testing and Assessment

       Arthur Coleman
       U. S. Department of Education

       • What federal protections are provided to English-language learning students under Titles I and VI?
       • What other federal initiatives seek to ensure that the rights of these students are protected?

4:30-5:30   Reactors:

       Charles Glenn
       Boston University

       Rebecca Zwick
       University of California, Santa Barbara

5:30-6:00   Discussion

6:00   Adjourn

Friday, October 15, 1999

8:30-9:15   **Federal Initiatives for English-Language Learning Students**

Moderator—Ulric Neisser, Cornell University

Judith Johnson
U. S. Department of Education

Rebecca Kopriva
U. S. Department of Education

• What federal initiatives seek to promote the educational opportunities of English-language learning students?

9:15-10:45   **State and Local Assessment of English-Language Learning Students**

Moderator—Diana Lam,
Providence School Department

Roseanne DeFabio
New York State Department of Education

Sonia Hernandez
California Department of Education

Merv Brennen
Illinois State Department of Education

• How are English-language learning students identified in the jurisdiction?
• To what content and performance standards are English-language learning students and their schools held accountable?
• What educational treatments are available to these students?
• For what purposes (instructional planning, system-level

monitoring and accountability, program placement or exit) and in what assessment domains (subject-matter knowledge, native language and literacy, English language and literacy, cognitive abilities) are English-language learning students tested in the jurisdiction?

- What are the policies and procedures for inclusion?
- What accommodations are offered?
- What happens to excluded students?
- How does the testing program report scores for individuals and groups?
- How do English-language learning students and their schools fare in standards-based testing in the jurisdiction?
- What is known about the validity of score data for English-language learning students?

10:45-11:00   Break

11:00-12:30   **State and Local Assessment of English-Language Learning Students (Continued)**

Maria Seidner
Texas Education Agency

Mary Ramirez
Philadelphia School District

Adel Nadeau
San Diego County Office of Education

12:30-1:15   Lunch

1:15-1:45   Discussion

1:45-2:15   **Commercial Testing Practices for English-Language Learning Students**

Moderator—Henry Levin, Columbia University

Maureen Grazioli
Riverside Publishing, ITBS

Margaret Jorgensen
Harcourt Educational Measurement, Stanford 9

Edward DeAvila
CTB/McGraw-Hill, TerraNova

2:15-3:15   Reactors:

Martin Carnoy
Stanford University

Marion Joseph
California Board of Education

3:15-3:45   Discussion/ Adjourn

WORKSHOP PARTICIPANTS

JAMAL ABEDI, University of California, Los Angeles, CRESST, *presenter*

DENNIS BEATRICE, SRI International

ALEXANDRA BEATTY, National Research Council

MERV BRENNAN, Illinois State Department of Education, *presenter*

MARTIN CARNOY, Stanford University, *presenter*

URSULA CASANOVA, Arizona State University, *presenter*

ARTHUR COLEMAN, Office for Civil Rights, U.S. Department of Education, *presenter*

EDWARD DEAVILA, CTB/McGraw-Hill, *presenter*

SHASHIKALA DEB, Cooley, Godward, LLP

ROSEANNE DEFABIO, New York State Department of Education, *presenter*

RICHARD DURAN, University of California, Santa Barbara, *presenter*

MICHAEL FEUER, National Research Council

CHARLES GLENN, Boston University, *presenter*

NORMAN GOLD, California Department of Education

MAUREEN GRAZIOLI, Riverside Publishing, *presenter*

KENJI HAKUTA, Stanford University, *presenter*

LARRY HEDGES, University of Chicago

SONIA HERNANDEZ, California Department of Education, *presenter*

JAY HEUBERT, Teachers College, Columbia University

CAROLYN HOFSTETTER, Policy Analysis for California Education

EUGENE JOHNSON, American Institutes for Research

JUDITH JOHNSON, Office of Elementary and Secondary Education, U.S. Department of Education, *presenter*

MARGARET JORGENSEN, Harcourt Educational Measurement, *presenter*

MARION JOSEPH, California Board of Education, *presenter*

JAMES KADAMUS, New York State Department of Education

REBECCA KOPRIVA, U.S. Department of Education, *presenter*

DIANA LAM, Providence School Department, Rhode Island

HENRY LEVIN, Teachers College, Columbia University

GOODWIN LIU, U.S. Department of Education

BARBARA MEANS, SRI International

KAREN MITCHELL, National Research Council

ADEL NADEAU, San Diego County Office of Education, *presenter*

ULRIC NEISSER, Cornell University

JAMES PELLEGRINO, Stanford University
DIANA PULLIN, Boston College
MARY RAMIREZ, Philadelphia School District, *presenter*
CHARLENE RIVERA, GWU Center for Equity and Excellence in Education, *presenter*
PETER SCHRAG, University of California, Berkeley
MARIA SEIDNER, Texas Education Agency, *presenter*
PATRICK SHIELDS, SRI International
ED SLAWSKI, Harcourt Educational Measurement
JIM STACK, San Francisco Unified School District
GWEN STEPHENS, California Department of Education
DAVID SWEET, U.S. Department of Education
WILLIAM TAYLOR, Attorney at Law, Board on Testing and Assessment, *presenter*
MARTHA THURLOW, University of Minnesota, *presenter*
JOHN TOBIN, Siemens Corporation, New York
WILLIAM TRENT, University of Illinois, Urbana-Champaign
REBECCA ZWICK, University of California, Santa Barbara, *presenter*

APPENDIX
B
Additional Resources

Abedi, Lord, Hofstetter, and Baker

in press Impact of Accommodation Strategies on English Language Learners' Test Performance, *Educational Measurement: Issues and Practices*.

Abedi, J., and C. Lord

in press Relationship between language background and performance in math. *Applied Measurement in Education*.

Abedi, J., and S. Leon

1999 *Impact of Students' Language Background on Content-Based Performance: Analyses of Extant Data*. Los Angeles: UCLA Center for the Study of Evaluation/National Center for Research on Evaluation, Standards, and Student Testing (CRESST).

Abedi, J., S. Leon, and J. Miracha

2000 *Impact of Students' Language Background on Content-Based Performance: Continued Analyses of Extant Data*. Los Angeles, CA: UCLA Center for the Study of Evaluation/National Center for Research on Evaluation, Standards, and Student Testing (CRESST).

Abedi, J., C.K. Boscardin, and H. Larson

2000 *AERA Special Interest Group: Summaries of Research on Inclusion of Students with Disabilities & Limited English Proficient Students in Large-Scale Assessments*. Los Angeles, CA: National Center for Research on Evaluation, Standards, and Student Testing.

Abedi, J., C. Hofstetter, C. Lord, and E. Baker

1998 *NAEP math performance and test accommodations: Interactions with student language background, Draft Report*. Los Angeles: University of California, Los Angeles, National Center for Research on Evaluation, Standards, and Student Testing (CRESST).

Anderson, N.E., F.F. Jenkins, and K.E. Miller
   1996   *NAEP Inclusion criteria and testing accommodations: Findings from the NAEP 1995 field-test in mathematics.* Washington, DC: Educational Testing Service.

Anstrom, K.
   1997   *Academic Achievement for Secondary Language Minority Students: Standards, Measures and Promising Practices.* Washington, DC: National Clearinghouse for Bilingual Education.

August, D., K. Hakuta, and D. Pompa
   1994   *For all students: Limited English Proficient Students and Goals 2000.* Washington, DC: National Clearinghouse for Bilingual Education.

August, D., and E. McArthur
   1996   *Proceedings of the Conference on Inclusion Guidelines and Accommodations for Limited English Proficient Students in National Assessment of Educational Progress.* NCES 96-861. Washington, DC: U.S. Department of Education, Office of Educational Research and Improvement.

Brennan, Mervin M.
   1995   *Illinois Teams Up: The New Illinois Alternative Assessment System for Limited English Proficient (LEP) Students.* Paper presented at the CCSSO Large Scale Assessment Conference in Phoenix, Arizona, on June 19, 1995.

Butler, F. A., and R. Stevens
   1997   *Accommodation Strategies for English Language Learners on Large-scale Assessments: Student Characteristics and Other Considerations CSE Technical Report 448.* Los Angeles: National Center for Research on Evaluation, Standards, and Student Testing (CRESST), University of California.

Figueroa, R.A., and S. Hernandez
   1999   A report to the nation: Testing hispanic students in the United States. For *Our Nation on the Fault Line: Hispanic American Education.* President's Advisory Commission on Educational Excellence for Hispanic Americans.

Kean, Michael H.
   1999   *Supporting Inclusive Assessment: A Publisher's Perspective.* Paper prepared for the NATD Symposium: Issues and Trends in Inclusive Assessment Practices held in Montreal, Canada, on April 20, 1999.

Lam, T.C., and W.I. Gordon
   1992   State policies for standardized achievement testing of limited English proficient students. *Educational Measurement: Issues and Practice* 11(4):18-20.

Lepik, M.
   1990   Algebraic word problems: Role of linguistic and structural variables. *Educational Studies in Mathematics* 21:83-90.

Mazzeo, J.
   1997   Toward a More Inclusive NAEP. Paper presented at the annual meeting of the American Educational Research Association, Chicago, IL.

Mazzeo, J.E., K.E. Carlson, Voelkl, and A.D. Lutkus
   2000   *Increasing the Participation of Special Needs Students in NAEP: A Report on 1996*

NAEP Research Activities. NCES 2000-473. Washington, DC: U.S. Department of Education, Office of Educational Research and Improvement.

Olson, J.F., and A.A. Goldstein

1997 *The Inclusion of Students with Disabilities and Limited English Proficiency Students in Large-Scale Assessments: A Summary of Recent Progress.* NCES 97-482. Washington DC: U.S. Department of Education, Office of Educational Research and Improvement.

Rivera, C., and C.W. Stansfield

1998 Leveling the playing field for English language learners: Increasing participation in state and local assessments through accommodations. In *Assessing Student Learning: New Rules, New Realities*, Ron Brandt, ed. Alliance for Curriculum Reform. Arlington, VA: Educational Research Service.

Shepard, L., G. Taylor, and D. Betebenner

1998 *Inclusion of Limited-English-Proficient Students in Rhode Island's Grade 4 Mathematics Performance Assessment.* CSE Tech. Rep. No. 486. Los Angeles, CA: National Center for Research on Evaluation, Standards, and Student Testing (CRESST), University of California.